A BOOK OF
WILDFLOWERS

BY
DR. WILLIAM A. NIERING

ILLUSTRATIONS BY ANITA MARCI

A FRIEDMAN GROUP BOOK

Published by GALLERY BOOKS
An imprint of W.H. Smith Publishers, Inc.
112 Madison Avenue
New York, New York 10016

ISBN 0-8317-9439-9

A BOOK OF WILDFLOWERS
was prepared and produced by
Michael Friedman Publishing Group, Inc.
15 West 26th Street
New York, NY 10010

Typeset by B.P.E. Graphics, Inc.
Color separations by Hong Kong Scanner Craft Company Ltd.
Printed and bound in Hong Kong by Leefung-Asco Printers Ltd.

CONTENTS

INTRODUCTION

This wildflower sampler is different from other such books in that it includes mostly species which occur in both North America and Europe. This does not imply that these plants have naturally evolved over this wide range but rather that man has played an integral part as disseminator. As Old World peoples migrated from Europe to the New World, the seeds of many of these species were inadvertently brought as contaminants in crop seed or in straw packing. These alien seeds found crop land and clearings ideal for their establishment and propagation. One need only walk into an untended vegetable garden or old field which has recently been agriculturally abandoned to attest to the success of these migrants. In my garden, celandine, black-eyed Susans, and buttercups are frequent "weeds," and in that part of my lawn which I have allowed to grow into an unmowed, grassy meadow, daisies, yarrow, and hawkweeds all thrive and add splashes of color throughout the summer.

Although most, if not all, of the wildflowers included here are really quite beautiful, as revealed by the superb artistry of Anita Marci, about half of them are considered weeds and are controlled by cultivation or herbicides where they occur in agriculture. This raises a most interesting question— what is a weed? It has been variously defined. Ralph Waldo Emerson suggested that it is a plant whose virtues have yet to be discovered. Others consider it a plant out of place. Sulphur cinquefoil and chickory would be colorful wildflowers in my meadow, but in a pasture or crop land they would be considered weeds.

Many weeds are highly cosmopolitan. For example, blue-weed occurs commonly as a plant in clearings or open fields and pastures in North America, Europe, and Australia. Typically, weeds are opportunistic species in that they take advantage of open disturbed sites where they do not have to compete too heavily with other species for space, sun, and water. They seldom threaten well-stabilized ecosystems within a given area. Some, however, like purple loosestrife, compete seriously with the native wetland flora in parts of North America. Man has not only played a major role in the geographical distribution of many of these plants, he has also helped to favor their continued occurrence.

Most of these wildflowers are perennials, which means that once established, they will automatically come up from year to year from the persisting root systems. Others, such as the evening primrose, form a rosette of basal leaves the first year followed by flowering and seed production in the second year after which the plant's roots die. A few are annuals which respond like the marigolds in our ornamental gardens. They must be started from seed each year and complete their life cycle in one year.

In addition to beautiful "weeds," this volume also includes some truly spectacular wildflowers such as orchids, irises, lilies, and columbines. These often occur as woodland spring wildflowers. Early flowering is a marvelous adaptation for taking advantge of the light available in spring before the forest canopy closes over for the summer.

Among the species in this primer, the pea and daisy families are best represented. Members of the pea family are ecologically important as nitrogen fixers. Their roots have the ability to take nitrogen from the soil and convert it into a usable source of nitrogen for the plant. When the plant dies, the soil is further enriched with nitrogen. The daisy family, one of the largest with over 20,000 species, has been most successful. This may be correlated with its highly evolved flower. Members of this family produce their flowers in heads in which many tiny florets are aggregated closely together so that when insect pollinators land many flowers are simultaneously pollinated. The tiny fruits or seeds of most of these flowers are dispersed as minute "parachutes" of fine bristles on wind currents.

As you enjoy this volume remember that this is but a sample of the more than 250,000 species of flowering plants that have evolved on our planet. Many of those included here may be just outside your door, even in an urban setting. May this be the beginning of an outdoor adventure that will lead to many hours of enjoyment searching for and identifying wildflowers.

William A. Niering

ACHILLEA

YARROW
(A. millefolium)
(Family: *Asteraceae*)

This is a pleasant aromatic plant with very striking fernlike leaves. The whitish gray, flat-topped flower clusters are composed of many separate flowers—yellowish central ones and whitish outer ones. The plant has been used in folk medicine to stop bleeding and tea brewed from its leaves is said to remedy colds. It is typically found along roadsides, in open fields, and in pastures. A closely related pink form, *A. lanulosa,* is planted in American gardens as an ornamental.

AQUILEGIA

COLUMBINE
(A. canadensis)
(Family: *Ranunculaceae*)

Columbine is a beautiful woodland flower found on rocky slopes and ledges. The five petals of the blossom form long spurs so that only long-tongued butterflies and moths can collect the sweet nectar within. Related to the common garden columbine, it is widely distributed in the eastern half of the United States, also extending into Canada, as the species name implies. Walking among the woodland boulders of New England in spring, one observer commented, "Every nook and cranny among them, and every little mat of earth upon them, is checkered with the flowery print of the Canada columbine."

CAMPANULA

HAREBELL

BLUEBELL

(C. rotundifolia)

(Family: *Campanulaceae*)

➤

Lovely, nodding, bell-like flowers on threadlike stalks
distinguish this member of the bluebell family.
Bumblebees are among the chief pollinators, and
they must clasp the stigma of the inverted flower to
enter, thus facilitating pollination. Campanula can be
found on rocky banks, in meadows, and near shores.
At high elevations it may have but a single flower.

CHRYSANTHEMUM

OX-EYE DAISY
(C. leucanthemum)
(Family: *Asteraceae*)

❧

You may be surprised to learn that this daisy is a *Chrysanthemum* related to the huge mums sold in flower shops. Typical of open clearings, they are among the showiest members of the daisy family. The flower head is a composite of flowers consisting of many individuals. Those tightly packed in the center form a "button" and are tube-shaped, whereas white straplike flowers—petallike in appearance—surround the yellow disk. The ornamentally lobed leaves also help to distinguish this old field wildflower.

CICHORIUM

CHICORY

SUCCORY

(C. intybus)

(Family: *Asteraceae*)

Chicory is a very beautiful roadside perennial with striking, true violet-blue blooms—a shade not common among flowers. These close in the rain but open in full sun. Five distinctive points at the end of each strap represent five fused petals, the corolla. The many individual straplike corollas that comprise each flower head are fascinating to study closely. Five fused stamens and a pistil are also present on each strap, making each a complete flower. The long taproot is dried and added to coffee to improve the flavor.

CYPRIPEDIUM

YELLOW LADY'S-SLIPPER

LADY'S-SLIPPER ORCHID

(C. calceolus)

(Family: *Orchidaceae*)

❧

The Latin name meaning "little shoe" is very appropriate, if a bit plain, for this showy orchid with a distinctive yellow sac forming one of its petals. The other two petals are brownish and spirally elongated. The Indians used the root in the treatment of parasitic worms. It grows in woods, thickets, bogs, and swamps. Cypripedium is a fine choice for the wild or bog garden.

CYTISSUS

BROOM
(C. scoparius)
(Family: *Fabaceae*)

❧

Covered with golden yellow, pealike blossoms, this erect stiff-stemmed shrub can reach 8 feet (2.5 m) in height. Its small leaves often fall, leaving the green stems bare. It is widespread in Europe where it can be found on heaths and in woodland clearings. A drug made from the twigs is used for heart and respiratory ailments, although the plant itself is poisonous to livestock. Branches are used for brooms, the plant having given its name to that housekeeping tool. It can coat whole landscapes with its yellow spikes. This is the flower that Wordsworth said "along the copses runs in veins of gold."

DAUCUS

QUEEN-ANNE'S LACE
WILD CARROT
(D. carota)
(Family: *Apiaeae*)

❧

This lacy, flat-topped flower cluster rivals any queen's lace in texture and beauty. Often there is a single, large, reddish purple flower in the center. It thrives in open fields or exposed ground. This hairy biennial was the ancestor of the garden carrot; its first-year taproot can be cooked and eaten. Although considered a weed, it is a most attractive addition to the informal, naturalistic garden.

DIANTHUS

DEPTFORD PINK
(D. armeria)
(Family: *Caryophyllaceae*)

This flower, with its five delicate, jagged-edged petals, resembles the garden flower Sweet William. The common name refers to Deptford, England, now a part of London, where the plant was once abundant. You can find this deep pink flower in fields or along hedgerows and roadsides. It is also called Lady's Cushion or Thrift.

DIGITALIS

FOXGLOVE
(D. purpurea)
(Family: *Scrophulariaceae*)

~

The nodding bell-shaped blossoms of this plant are especially ornamental. The Latin name refers to the fingerlike flowers. Although grown in gardens, foxglove frequently escapes into the wild and is widely distributed in temperate regions of the world. In New Zealand I have even seen them growing wild along the coast near Nelson. An important drug, digitalin, obtained from the leaves, is used to slow down the rate of heart beat. It is a difficult medicinal plant, though, as slightly too large a dose can prove a deadly poison.

EPILOBIUM

FIREWEED
WILLOW-HERB
ROSEBAY
(E. angustifolium)
(Family: *Onagraceae*)

Fireweed's flowers are distinctively four-parted, and the ovary gives rise to an attractive, long and slender fruit. When ripe, these fruits split open and discharge large numbers of seeds with silky parachutes which can be carried long distances by the wind. Fireweed is often the first plant to colonize burn sites, transforming the blackened landscape into a sea of pink.

EPIPACTIS

BROAD HELLEBORINE
(E. helleborine)
(Family: *Orchidaceae*)

~

This is a large orchid reaching 4 feet (1.2 meters) in height. Its drooping, scentless flowers tend to occur along one side of the flowering stalk. Individual blossoms with their little saclike lips merit close examination. The large, spirally arranged leaves have conspicuous veins and are often over 6 inches (15 cm) in length. Found in woods and thickets and along streamsides, this is the only orchid known to have been introduced to North America from Europe.

ERODIUM

COMMON STORKSBILL

ALFILARIA

(E. cicutarium)

(Family: *Geraniaceae*)

～

The plant takes its common names from the long, beaklike capsules which are its fruits. The leaves resemble a fern's leaves, and the small, light purple flowers rise on long stalks in groups of two to nine. Storksbill is common from early spring to mid-autumn throughout Great Britain and North America. In the western United States—where it is also called by the picturesque names Filaree and Clocks—it will bloom as early as February. Storksbill prefers clearings, roadsides, fields, and dunes, growing even in the Sonoran desert of the American Southwest. Surprisingly, it is a member of the geranium family.

HABENARIA

PURPLE-FRINGED ORCHID
(H. fimbriata)
(Family: *Orchidaceae*)

❧

One of the petals of this orchid is highly modified, forming a deeply fringed lip, and spurred. Nectar accumulates in the spur. Butterflies and moths are the chief pollinators. As they search for nectar, pollen often gets picked up and carried to another flower. This is one of the most strikingly beautiful wild orchids in North America. The purplish lilac flowers make a gorgeous addition to the bog garden, though the plant demands a very acid soil.

HIERACIUM

ORANGE HAWKWEED

DEVIL'S PAINTBRUSH

(H. aurantiacum)

(Family: *Asteraceae*)

An expanse of orange hawkweed in bloom along a roadside or in an open field can be breathtaking. In spite of its loveliness, however, it is considered a pernicious weed. The blackish hairs on the bracts around the flower heads and elsewhere are a distinctive feature. A sixteenth-century herbalist indicated that due to the likeness of these hairs to coal dust, women named the plant Grim the Collier.

Its symmetrical heads are composed solely of straplike flowers and arise from a set of basal leaves.

HYPERICUM

COMMON ST. JOHNSWORT
(H. perforatum)
(Family: *Hypericaceae*)

A native of Asia, this plant has become successfully naturalized in Europe and North America where it is common in fields and along roadsides. The yellow flowers, with their numerous stamens, are very showy. The small, opposite, ovate leaves have translucent dots visible when held up to the light.

The common name is derived from St. John's Eve—June 24—when the plant blooms. Folk legends say the leaves develop red spots on August 29, the day the saint was beheaded. The suffix '-wort' meant medicinal herb in Anglo-Saxon, and the plant has had endless uses in herbal medicine. It was even supposed to cure madness, though tradition says that anyone treading on it after dark will be wheeled through the heavens all night on the back of a magical horse.

IRIS

YELLOW FLAG
(I. pseudacorus)
(Family: *Iridaceae*)

Introduced from the Old World to American gardens, this showy iris has escaped from cultivated gardens and is now naturalized in many wetlands. It is also frequently found along river marshes. Swordlike leaves distinguish the members of the iris group. The flowers are unique in form with three backward-curving sepals and three upright petals. Beneath the three arching stigma over the sepals are three hidden stamens. The brown fruits (capsules) may be used in dried flower arrangements. Other local names for it include Dragon Flower, and for its leaves, Dagger Flower.

LILIUM

MARTAGON LILY
(L. martagon)
(Family: *Liliaceae*)

The spectacular nodding blossoms occur in clusters of three to ten. The flowers are a fleshlike pink or pale purple, mottled with darker spots. Petals and petallike sepals are strongly reflexed. It is found throughout Europe in woods and thickets. This is a sequel to the Turk's cap lily, *L. superbum,* found in North America.

LINARIA

TOADFLAX
BUTTER AND EGGS
(L. vulgaris)
(Family: *Scrophulariaceae*)

~

The spikelike masses of linaria's two-toned yellow-orange flowers resemble a small version of the garden snapdragon, to which they are related. The orange patch on the lower lip of the petals serves as a honey guide for insect pollinators, especially bumblebees. Nectar collects in the long spur, which can be easily reached by moths with their long tongues. In Germany the flowers are used for making yellow dyes. Linaria is commonly found in dry open habitats such as fields and roadsides. Toads are said to enjoy the shade beneath its leaves, but the common name toadflax may come from a misreading, the Latin for "useful" having been taken for the word for "toad." In fact, the plant has been used in folk medicine to cure everything from boils to jaundice.

LYTHRUM

PURPLE LOOSESTRIFE
SPIKED WILLOW-HERB
LONG PURPLES
SPIKED LOOSESTRIFE
(L. salicaria)
(Family: *Lythraceae*)

～

In large numbers, the magenta flowers of purple loosestrife can provide a striking spectacle in wet meadows or marshes. Loosestrife has become such an aggressive alien in parts of the northeastern United States that there is concern that native wetland species will be crowded out. The plant responds well to cultivation and makes an attractive addition to any perennial garden. And it has had endless uses in folk medicine and custom. The ancients reportedly strung garlands of it around the necks of plowing oxen, to make them docile in the fields. The plants have been burned as an insect repellant, and extracts from them were once used to color hair blond. A drug derived from loosestrife is still used today in the treatment of amoebic dysentery.

MENYANTHES

BOGBEAN BUCKBEAN
(M. trifoliata)
(Family: *Menyanthaceae*)

Among the most beautiful of marsh plants, buckbean sends up tall stems adorned all along their lengths with lovely white and red flowers. Each has hairy nodes along the inside of its petals, lending the whole bloom a slightly unearthly quality. Found in bogs, marshes, and on the edges of lakes and ponds, buckbean blooms from late spring to late summer. Even today, herbal doctors use it in the treatment of colds and fevers. In olden days, it was also used to cure scurvy and, as one authority put it, to treat "hot rotten agues."

OENOTHERA

EVENING PRIMROSE
(O. biennis)
(Family: *Onagraceae*)

➤

As the common name implies, these flowers suddenly open in the evening and usually close by noon. For this reason, they are also known as Evening Star. The flowers have four petals and eight prominent stamens. The pollen is connected by cobwebby threads which make it easier for moths to transport. As a biennial it takes two years to flower, and then the plant dies. The cooked root can be eaten and resembles parsnip, but it must be collected at the right time. If taken too early or late it has a peppery taste. The oil of evening primrose has recently appeared as a cosmetic. Taken in pill form, it is said to help prevent aging of the skin.

POTENTILLA

SULPHUR CINQUEFOIL
ROUGH-FRUITED CINQUEFOIL
(R. recta)
(Family: *Rosaceae*)

～

An attractive member of the rose family, this cinquefoil makes a broad, simple flower whose color bleeds from sulphur yellow to cream. Each bloom has a lovely nest of stamens at its heart, and the flowers appear in spare clusters on long, hairy stems. In reduced form, the Sulphur Cinquefoil shares some of the elegance of the cultivated rugosa roses. It grows in dry fields and along roadsides from late spring through high summer. Originally introduced from Central Europe, it is found naturalized in England and in quantities in Eastern and Midwestern North America. Nebraska farmers loathe it as a weed in their pastures.

RANUNCULUS

BULBOUS BUTTERCUP

(R. bulbosus)

(Family: *Ranunculaceae*)

～

This is one of several showy Old World buttercups. The distinctively waxy texture of the shiny yellow petals is the result of a special layer of cells found just beneath the surface. This species is recognized by its bulbous base or root. Common in fields and meadows, it is poisonous to livestock. It has been used in poultices to help heal rashes, but the herbalist Gerard warned against careless use of the *Ranunculus* in herbal medicine, for, as he put it, "they are of a most violent force." Surprisingly to some, the buttercups are not native to Europe: they were brought back from Turkey and the Levant by returning Crusaders.

ROSA

PRICKLY ROSE
ALBERTA ROSE
(R. acicularis)
(Family: *Rosaceae*)

Few flowers are as hardy or as widely distributed as the prickly rose. Its lovely, solitary rose-pink blossoms appear on a dense and very spiny bush that grows up to about 4 feet (1.2 meters) high. And the plant bears very pretty, pear-shaped red hips once the flowers are gone. Its range covers the whole northern third of the United States and all of Canada, from the Adirondacks of New York to the province of New Brunswick. It also grows wild in the mountains of Mongolia, the Kuriles, and Japan. Its hardiness has won it the nickname arctic rose, and it is the provincial flower of Alberta. The prickly rose has been naturalized in Britain since early in the nineteenth century.

SAPONARIA

BOUNCING BET
SOAPWORT
(S. officinalis)
(Family: *Caryophyllaceae*)

❧

Bouncing Bet is a showy white or pink phloxlike fragrant flower that has come to America from Europe. The petals are scalloped with small appendages. This plant may be used for washing hands, as it contains a soaplike substance (saponins) which lathers when the foliage is crushed. One of the common names, Bouncing Bet, refers to the appearance of a washerwoman, Betty, using an old-fashioned washing board.

TANACETUM

COMMON TANSY

(T. vulgare)

(Family: *Asteraceae*)

The flat-topped clusters of the tansy's buttonlike heads are composed of many tiny flowers but lack the typical collar of straplike flowers, a characteristic of tansy's relative, the daisies. The name of this highly aromatic plant comes from Old French *tonesie,* derived from the Greek word *athanasia,* meaning immortality. In ancient times, it was wrapped in winding sheets and rubbed on corpses, perhaps to insure them a place in the afterlife. The plant has been useful in folk medicine for many of man's ills. A tea brewed from its leaves has been used for curing aches and pains.

TRICHOSTEMA

BLUE CURLS

(T. dichotomum)

(Family: *Lamiaceae*)

The name Blue Curls refers to the extraordinarily long, curled stamens that form beautiful curves far beyond the petals of this two-lipped flower. It is a low-growing annual found in dry, open, sandy areas and along roadsides. In California, it grows much taller. There, this attractive member of the mint family is valued also for its attractiveness to bees.

TRIFOLIUM

RABBIT-FOOT CLOVER

(T. arvense)

(Family: *Fabaceae*)

❧

The elongated flowering heads of this clover resemble the furry feet of rabbits. This furry appearance comes from tiny hairs on the sepals of the small, greenish white flowers. A low-growing annual, it is often found in open fields or on bare soil areas. As a member of the Pea family, it has tripartite and cloverlike leaves.

TRIFOLIUM

RED CLOVER
(T. pratense)
(Family: *Fabaceae*)

This is an important forage plant on both sides of the Atlantic, especially where the spring climate is cool. It, like other legumes, has the ability to fix atmospheric nitrogen, a process which occurs in tiny nodules on the roots. If you examine a red clover, wash the soil from its roots and study these valuable structures. Red clover and other related legumes, like alfalfa, serve as important cover crops and improve soil fertility. Trifolium means three-leaved, and during medieval times, the triple sprigs were valued as a charm against witches.

TRILLIUM

LARGE-FLOWERING TRILLIUM
(T. grandiflorum)
(Family: *Liliaceae*)

～

This is a large-flowered trillium that often finds its way into wildflower gardens. The three waxy white petals are larger than the three outer green sepals and turn pink with age. It can be found in rich woods from Missouri to Minnesota and northward into Canada. This trillium is the provincial flower of Ontario.

VERBASCUM

COMMON MULLEIN
(V. thapsus)
(Family: *Scrophulariaceae*)

❧

This common stout biennial, frequently found in waste places, banks, and clearings, can attain a height of 8 feet (2.4 meters). Its rosette of velvety, hairy leaves and its tightly packed spike of slightly asymmetrical yellow flowers are its distinguishing features. Roman soldiers are known to have used the flowering stalks for torches after dipping them in grease. The woolly leaves have been used for tea, wicks, and as padding to keep feet warm. Before rouge, women used the leaves to redden cheeks by rubbing the fuzzy leaf on the skin and irritating it. The masses of delicate, branched leaf hairs of the plant are most unusual and well worth examining with a hand lens.

WILDFLOWERS IN THE GARDEN

While many of the flowers in this book are at their best in the wild, a number of them make fine additions to the wild, or naturalistic, garden.

Aquilegia

The columbines are difficult to grow. They tend to look flabby in the garden, and they interbreed easily, producing unsightly offspring. But if you can grow true seed of *A. canadensis* for your rock garden, you will have a lovely plant indeed. Plant it in clumps, preferably in full sun, in rocky soil.

Campanula

Growing in the grass, in the rock garden, or in a flower border, *C. rotundifolia* gives a lovely effect. Easy to grow from seed or by division, this campanula has only one problem: it may become rampant.

Cypripedium

Cypripediums can be difficult to grow in the garden, though surpassingly lovely. Fortunately, *C. calceolus* is among the easiest. It may grow in rich garden earth, but the best idea is to give it a limy soil enriched with leaf mold. Make sure it has plenty of shade by planting taller bushes to protect it, if necessary.

Daucus

Queen-Anne's Lace (*D. carota*) is virtually a symbol of the wild and is easy to grow. It graces many a woodland bouquet or flower arrangement in late summer.

Epilobium

Fireweed (*E. angustifolium*) is a spectacular flower. When planted in masses, it can be seen from quite far off. Place it in open woodland settings, where its rampant growth will not disturb the rest of the garden.

Habenaria

The orchids of this genus are difficult to grow, and they seldom last more than a season or two. Still, they are so beautiful that it is worth a try, if you have a bog or woodland site. Grow them in half-shade in a moist, peaty soil.

Iris

All the irises make gardens shine, but Yellow Flag (*I, pseudacoris*) gives a specially wild and pleasant effect. They should be planted in a sunny location with limy soil.

Lilium

William Robinson recommends the planting of various species of the lilies as accent plants in the rhododendron garden. *L. superbum* is particularly recommended for the bog or woodland garden.

Lythrum

Purple loosestrife (*L. salicaria*) adapts very well to the cultivated perennial garden. It looks especially well, besides, gracing the edge of a pond. Try the variety called *L. roseum superbum*.

Oenothera

Handsome and hardy, the evening primrose (*O. biennis*) will grow in almost any soil. Plant it out of the way of the rest of the garden, however, as it spreads very freely.

Saponaria

Soapwort (*S. officinalis*) was suggested by William Robinson for the rock or heath garden, but he reports no results.

Trillium

The trillium pictured in this volume is the most beautiful of a wide genus. Plant it in masses in a shady area of moist soil enriched with leaf mold. Propagate by seed or by rhizomes.

WILDFLOWER GLOSSARY

ALTERNATE
Having one leaf at every stem node, pointing in different directions.

ANNUAL
A plant that completes its life cycle (germinates, grows, flowers, fruits, and dies) within a single year or growing season.

ANTHER
The saclike, upper part of the stamen where pollen is produced. When the anther breaks, wind or insects carry pollen to the tip of the pistil.

APPENDAGE
Any subsidiary part attached to another part.

AXIL
The angle formed where a leaf or branch diverges from the stem or axis to which it is attached.

BASAL LEAVES
Leaves that grow at the base of the stem.

BEARDED
Bearing hairs, either stiff or elongated.

BISEXUAL
Said of flowers having both stamens (male) and pistils (female) on a single flower.

BLADE
The flat part of a sepal, petal or leaf.

BRACT
A small, leaflike, occasionally brightly colored organ usually located at the base of the flower.

BULB
A subterranean organ made up of tightly packed leaves.

CALYX
The collective term for the sepals, which form the outer whorl of the flower.

CAPSULE
A dry fruit that releases its seed through slits or pores.

CARPEL
The female organ of a flower, comprised of stigma, style and ovary.

COMPOUND
Referring to a leaf divided into smaller leaflets arranged either in two rows (pinnate) or radially, like a fan (palmate).

COROLLA
The collective term for the petals which form the inner whorl of the flower.

CORYMB
A panicle, all of whose flowers are arranged roughly along the same plane.

CYME
A wide, usually branching cluster of flowers, in which a bloom appears at the end of each stalk.

DISK FLOWER
The tiny tubular flowers at the center of a tight flower head, as in daisies.

DISTURBED SITE
Any area of ground that has previously been cleared or excavated for human purposes.

DIVIDED
Referring to a deeply cut leaf, the cleft not reaching to the central vein.

EXOTIC
Of plants that are not native; from another region.

FILAMENT
The stalk connected to the anther in a stamen.

HEAD
A tight cluster of flowers, each on a very short stalk or even stalkless.

HERBACEOUS
A soft-stemmed plant; not woody.

HIP
The fruit of a rose.

LEAFLET
Each leaflike part of a compound leaf.

LEGUME
A fruit developed from a single ovary, usually splitting at maturity into two valves, as in the Pea family.

LIP
The lower petal of asymmetrical flowers, as in orchids.

LOBED
Indented, but not divided into separate parts.

OPPOSITE
Having a pair of leaves at each stem node.

OVARY
The swollen, lower portion of the pistil that produces tiny ovules, which, following fertilization, develop into seeds.

OVATE
In the shape of an egg, pointed at the top.

PALMATE
Lobed like the fingers of a hand.

PERENNIAL
A plant that lasts through more than two growing seasons.

PERIANTH
A flower's nonsexual, outer parts, either as a tube or as calyx and corolla.

PETAL
The inner segments of the perianth; basic units of the corolla, surrounding the flower's reproductive organs.

PINNATE
Said of leaves appearing in opposite pairs along a central stalk, in the manner of a feather.

PISTIL
The female organ of a flower, consisting of stigma, style, and ovary.

POLLEN
Spores produced in the anthers, carrying the male reproductive elements.

RACEME
An elongated flower branch with stalked flowers.

RAY FLOWER
In the Daisy family, the bilaterally symmetrical flowers around the edge of the head; each flower resembles a petal.

REFLEXED
Term used to describe leaves and petals that bend backwards.

RHIZOME
A creeping underground rootstock which sprouts each year anew.

ROSETTE
A dense, circular cluster of leaves usually appearing at the base of a stem; it often seems to grow right out of the ground.

RUGOSE
Wrinkled.

RUNNER
A stem that grows along the ground, sending out new roots and plants at the nodes or tip.

SAC
A bag-shaped structure in a plant.

SCALLOPED
Having shallow, rounded projections.

SCORPIOID
A coiled flower cluster with the flowers usually appearing on one side of the stem.

SEPAL
Part of the calyx of a flower, usually green, but sometimes brightly colored; hence, they are sometimes mistaken for petals where true petals are absent.

SIMPLE
Said of a leaf with no divisions in the blade.

SPADIX
A thick spike of tiny flowers, usually enclosed in a spathe.

SPIKE
An elongated flower branch with stalkless flowers.

SPUR
A hollow, slender projection from the flower base.

STAMEN
The male pollen producing organ of a flower, consisting of a filament topped by an anther.

STANDARD
The upper petal, or banner, of members of the Pea family; the iris petal.

STIGMA
The usually divided or club-shaped tip of the pistil, which receives pollen.

STYLE
The part of the pistil which joins the ovary to the stigma.

TAPROOT
The strongly developed central root of a plant, usually extending straight down.

TENDRIL
A coiling structure that helps support climbing plants.

TUBER
The fleshy part of a subterranean stem, for storage of nutrients.

UMBEL
A flower cluster whose individuals have stalks growing from a single point.

WHORL
At a stem node, a circle of leaves, branches, or flowers.

WOODY
Said of plants with wooden, as opposed to fleshy, stems; not herbaceous.